SUBLIMATE

by
J. M. Tolcher

SUBLIMATE © 2025 by J. M. Tolcher. All rights reserved. No part of this book may be used or reproduced in any manner whatsoever without written permission except in the case of brief quotations embodied in critical articles and reviews.

First Edition published 2025.

ISBN 978-1-7636813-1-6

Cover: Ryan Smidt and James Tolcher

For Piggy.
The dry season is over.

"There goes another novel."
     — Honoré de Balzac, after ejaculation

"Ars totum requirit hominem!"
"[The art requires the whole person!]"
     — the old alchemists

The following book was written and edited under certain ejaculatory conditions.

While every attempt was made for this book to be self-contained so that it may be read and enjoyed as an individual work, the narrative does contain some minor references to characters and events in *Poof*.

CONTENTS

A Note on the Psychological Definition of Sublimation

—

	Prologue - Day 1	17
I	*Albedo*	23
	Intermission - Day 28	71
II	*Citrinitas*	77
	Intermission - Day 35	111
III	*Rubedo*	115
	Epilogue - Day X	119

—

A Note on the Psychological Definition of Sublimation

It started with Sigmund Freud who claimed that sublimation was the necessary process through which society was maintained. Hermann Hesse wrote to Carl Jung asking about this process of sublimation, and in his response, Jung attacked Freud, saying that Freud had misappropriated sublimation from the old alchemists, to whom sublimation meant the quest for the philosopher's stone and the creation of gold from the lowest and basest materials. Jung argued that Freud's twisted version of sublimation was nothing but repression—and that Freud gifted this tactic to the bourgeoisie to keep down the common man. Freud's student, Wilhelm Reich, knew this. To distance himself from Freud, he renamed what Freud called Eros to his own theory of Orgone, declaring that it was libido that governed the universe—and that libido must not be repressed, for it is repression of libido that causes illness and neuroses. It was a perfectly sensible theory with a perfectly sensible antagonist—what Reich called The Emotional Plague and diagnosed as authoritarian societies being crushed under the weight of their own armour. And then, I'm not one for conspiracy theories, but Reich seemed to go insane immediately after his perfect diagnosis, as if falling to an invisible enemy... But then Erich Fromm agreed, stating that it was repressed masochism, neurotic masochism, that gives rise to fascism. And as an adolescent I had a sense of all this and thought, well, if I am required to be masochistic, I will be the most masochistic of all—and that will teach me the ways of my sadistic enemies, and hopefully free me from them, though it will require seducing them, and loving them, and I did not know just how agonising that would be, and what parts of myself would be left behind. And the more I have learned, the more I think Reich was correct, that the plague we fight can be defeated with authenticity, truth, and rationality. I need not even fight it directly. It is enough to simply live, without repressing those dark parts of myself but making them sublime.

One mystery Wilhelm Reich did note was that in orgasm,

"the organism unceasingly attempts to bring together the two embryologically important zones, the mouth and the anus." This is no mystery. What is the symbol of the mouth and the tail meeting? It is ouroboros, of course. It is why the French call the orgasm *la petit mort*—the little death. The end and the new beginning. And that nascent libido which is so exciting, if you let it: what will it be this time?

Day 1

The first thing I suppose I ought to explain to you is the nature of my antagonist — or at least what I already know about him.

For example, if I were the kind of man that had a sex addiction requiring compulsive releases five times a day, that compulsion might lend some urgency to the task in front of me and explain why you are holding only a very thin novella in your hands, likely completed in about forty-five minutes.

Alternatively, if I were a eunuch, you may very well be struggling to hold up an encyclopaedic tome that had intricately come to fruition over the course of my long, cumless life.

Alas, let me tell you that I am somewhere in the middle.

See, I must have been quite young when I learned that pleasure mostly existed in the wanting of something and that desire vanished upon fulfillment.

It may have been a combination of some confused notions on suffering and my first sexual experience with an older teenage neighbour when I was just a boy, him wrestling me down and playing with me when I was pinned, that had me curious about denial — or maybe I am hard-wired like the Catholics.

Either way, I felt definitively empty and irritable following a self-given ejaculation as a teenager, to the point where sometimes I would manage to make it as long as a month or two between releases.

On average, however, it would only be a couple of days, and, being so pent up, usually once I had released once I could not stop myself from going again and again and again, and it might take eight ejaculations and a wasted afternoon of self-exploration before I finally quit.

But the point is that, from early on I was practicing self-discipline, and that combined with my initial wrestling experience (and maybe many other experiences that shaped me) led to a bondage and discipline fetish, which led to me being a submissive boy throughout my twenties and a lot of time wearing a chastity device for dominant men.

I think my record for wearing that device was about six weeks.

I found that the first four weeks are difficult and exciting, though after a month of wear, I started to wonder what the point of it all was.

My mentality may have been different if I had a suitable "Dominant" to give myself to, though the only men I ever met who saw themselves that way and with whom I had a genuine sexual spark had the unfortunate commonality of wanting to dominate others to replace and avoid understanding (or dominating) themselves.

The result was they failed to have a true grasp on human nature and could not sustain the depth of relationship I sought, and it was ultimately pointless to refrain from orgasms because there was no one to please.

I couldn't help the feeling that my boyhood was wasted on an idiotic population where not one man knew how to make the most of me.

Despite that, I have had some fun forging the path to the truth of human desire (at least my own) and testing its limits.

Given my experience in this area, I had the idea for attempting to write an entire book without cumming.

This is what I am setting out to do.

I considered postponing it to time the commencement of it immediately following an ejaculation, though I felt like that level of planning constituted some form of cheating the system or the universe, and that I must make the sincerest attempt (come success or failure) within the same window of time that the concept entered my mind.

I thought this was also the best way to honour you as a reader.

What good is writing a book under these conditions if the writer has it all planned out and knows exactly what they are going to write?

No, I had to start immediately.

I debated what to do about it since I wanted to complete another novel that I had already started.

I suppose I must have decided to abandon that other project (for now) and commence this one, because here I am writing it instead.

I

Albedo

I suppose it starts like last time.

You are thirty-two and it is your third Mardi Gras. You are getting your cock sucked in the bathroom and doing—what is it this time—coke, ketamine, GHB, molly? —All of the above.

Piggy is making animal noises, bleating like a sacrificial goat. People in the other stalls are laughing. But when you open the stall door, surprise, there's another security guard ready to give you the shakedown.

"I know what you were doing in there," the guard says. "I was standing here the whole time."

"You heard my animal noises?" Piggy starts up with the bleating again, doesn't realise he's in trouble, thinks security just wants his autograph or something— (you'd expect a fifty-year-old senior executive to have more sense, honestly)—but that might work, you think, since you've got all the drugs, and you sidle by, walking away, maybe he won't—

"Come back here!" security yells.

You turn around, acting just as confused and innocent as Piggy.

"Hmm? What's up?" you say, wide-eyed, as if this is the first you've noticed him.

"I know you were snorting coke in there. I heard everything. Don't try to deny it. So just hand it over and I won't have to take you to the police."

He leads you into the darkness outside the bathroom.

The trick with shakedowns is not to shake, and Piggy, now that he's half-caught on to the situation, starts shaking big time. He's getting emotional. Angry.

"What's your problem? It's Mardi Gras! Let people have fun!" He's leaning in for a fight. Not a good tactic when you have a bag full of drugs. Security grins, reckons he has the two of you by the balls. You try to get in between them, both big men at least twice your size.

"Piggy! Shush! Hey!—"

"You weren't even there for that long!" yells Piggy, trying to get around you. "Did you *hear* my animal noises? Because if you didn't you weren't there that long!"

"HEY! Be quiet! Can I handle this, please?"

Piggy finally looks you in the eye and goes quiet.

"Thank you." You turn to the security guard. He's big and fat, you know the type, thinks his size gives him power and that a "kid like you" (you can hear his thoughts) is too stupid to get away with anything, which suits you perfectly.

"I know what this looks like," you say, "but honestly, we were just fucking in there. If I had coke, I would give it to you, but I can't give you what I don't have."

Your demeanour is easy.

Non-confrontational.

Not even a glimmer of panic.

Brave when you're wearing nothing but a jockstrap and said bag full of drugs.

Piggy is still trying to argue ethics over your shoulder as if this security guard gives a shit about law-and-order and doesn't just want your cocaine, every-man-for-himself, and if he doesn't get it he's got nothing to lose in turning you into the on-site police. You're truly the only one that ever has any decorum.

And this would be so much easier to manage if you could explain to Piggy that you're being asked for a bribe and that he's not in court yet, but you can't explain that in front of the security guard or he'll get the picture that you're not the ditzy little idiot boy he still thinks you are.

Now, what are you going to do?

You're not getting arrested, and more importantly, you're not giving up the coke.

You're also definitely not getting kicked out this time.

You manage to shut Piggy up again but security is not buying your story that all that went on in that bathroom was hot and pure, innocent, drug-free, man-on-man hole pillaging. How else can you convince him? It occurs to you that you've got an empty baggy…

"If I had some… I would give it to you—" you say, rummaging around in your bag until you find it, "but we don't have cocaine. Okay, we might have done some pills, but they're all finished… see, I'll show you…"

You whip out the empty baggy to show him, triumphant.

Except that's not the empty baggy. That's the gram of coke.

And he's seen it.

But in a second it's switched hands, the other hand tucking it into the back of your jockstrap, your original hand whisking out—where is that goddamn empty baggy?!—

"Hey! What was that? Show me that!" says the security, who, I mean, you're still not phased by this guy. You really come alive in these moments.

"Yeah?"

You present the empty baggy to him. Same hand. Not a second later. Like a magic trick. You're a genius.

Except, fuck, that one's not empty either.

Both of you stare at the baggy in front of you, in it a single lonely MDMA cap. At this point you're basically just presenting your wares.

"Oh my god, I guess we had one left! I had no idea. I'm really sorry, I would *never* lie to you!" You lay it on thick like you believe this guy really is just doing his job and all he cares about is for everyone to have a safe, drug-free event. "Here, take this, it's all we have left anyway."

He takes the baggy with the molly and you can tell he's satisfied. You're almost in the clear when you feel the coke slip out of your jockstrap onto the floor and you've got to find a way to pick it up right in front of him. You slide a pack of gum out of your bag and throw it on the ground.

"Whoops!"

"What was that?!" he shines his torch at the floor, searching in the direction of the gum. You look down, locate the baggy while he's distracted, place your foot over it.

"Just my gum. Silly me."

He growls.

"Well, thanks!" you say, "have a great night!"

You bend down to grab the coke and the gum. Piggy's standing there like now it's *his* turn to go one-on-one with security, but you get right in his face before he can re-incriminate you. "Go. Now." He can tell you're serious and not to argue. You manage to get him downstairs where he's scathing mad.

"What the fuck! He took our cap!"

"Who cares about a cap? If that was up to you, we would be getting *arrested* right now. Don't you remember me writing about this exact same thing happening last time? I pretended I was 16 and didn't have ID?"

"No—what?"

He's shaking his head at you. The party is loud and you're both high. He has no conception of what just went on.

"We're still at the party and we still have the coke. Trust me. That was a good outcome. When I tell you about this tomorrow…"

You dance all night, fuck him under the bleachers. Dawn comes, the sun shines its first rays on the crowd of naked bodies still dancing, and this might be the happiest you've ever felt.

You walk home, traffic beeping, "looking good boys!" someone shouts, tie him to the bed, and at some point, with your cock down his throat, you feel like something has ended, like now you're a man. Capable and alive and here.

A strange sensation. Like you're becoming someone new. Who?

And what am *I* doing here? I mean, you call me in to help with creating some of your own "law and order," build this new version of yourself, a little bit of Apollo to balance out all that excess and partying but look at the story so far… At some point I'm just enabling you.

So what's the plan? To write a whole book without having an orgasm? And that's going to help you discover who you are—what part you play?

That's how this all began, isn't it?

You were invited to Sydney for a seven-hour stage production about the modern lives of gay men. It drew the attention of your friends who thought that your life, your last book, would be well reenacted in theatre, and that two of the lead actors would be perfect for the parts—one that apparently resembled you closely, the other, a daddy-type, a good fit for the whole cast of men who betrayed or let you down. You're not so sure that you want to spend any more time thinking about your past, but you come to see the play anyway.

You watch as the boy who you are told "looks just like you" acts out two characters: the first, an actor who everything goes just right for, makes it to Broadway and assumedly riches and fame, but then, next, he takes on the role of a down-and-out writer, used by wealthy and powerful men for his young body, and then discarded. These two characters are mistaken for one another—the writer is used and hurt even more for his resemblance to the actor.

You were meant to meet one of the actors after the show, a friend of a friend, but he was sick. In your bag is a signed copy of your first book for him, so you approach some of the cast members who are in the lobby, and as you do, a man chatting with them reaches out his hand.

"Congratulations! Well done! Amazing performance!" he beams at you.

He has confused you, the ravaged writer, for the successful actor in the play—the actor who not moments ago was playing both your parts.

Quod est superius est sicut quod inferius, et quod inferius est sicut quod est superius.

"Thank you," you say, "but that wasn't me."

"Well, maybe you'll have something else I can congratulate you for," says the man.

"Maybe this."

You pull out your book, explaining that you were meant to meet the actor who is sick, and that this was a gift for him. One of the cast members takes the book and agrees to pass it along to him.

You wish them goodnight.

You walk down the street with a sensation that the theatricalities have not come to an end.

You wonder what happens to the writer after the play, after the story is told.

The moment feels pregnant with something that you have no idea how to work with. You feel like a passive puppet, reading your lines, standing on your marks. What's interesting about that?

One scene from the play lingers in your mind: E. M. Forster being accosted for not having the courage to publish *Maurice*, a manuscript he kept hidden, a manuscript which so delicately and beautifully told the truth of gay men's lives. Forster was not courageous enough to publish *Maurice*, let alone become Maurice. Even that story is a distorted reflection of your own life: a wealthy man who throws it all away to be with his lover who has nothing to his name. But Forster did not have that bravery, just as so many of the men in your life were cowards, too scared to risk their façades for you, those façades of heavy iron and steel, weighing themselves down with armour, too scared to take a blow. Maybe that book was too idealistic. But here you are, your own book in hand, like a magical sword, saving the world (getting ahead of yourself?). A sword and no armour. That's the way to live. You find that you can't resent Forster, can't be mad at him. What for? What is it they want from that dead author, you wonder? Permission to live? Is that something a dead author can give? Maybe. Why don't they just give it to themselves? You had to. Well, that's the start of an answer: you're someone who tries to give yourself permission… and following that, to give it to everyone else too. Very like me. Authoritative. Someone must print the licenses—why not you? We need a new boss around here. Just look at the security—I don't think their hearts are in it at all.

Besides, who do you need to convince before you'll allow yourself to live? Your friends? Your enemies? Your leaders? Me?—am I the god of life? Try Eros. I can give you order but I cannot give you yourself, unrestricted.

Then, say you do manage to corner that elusive person, how are you going to convince them that you deserve freedom?

("Can you persuade us if we refuse to listen?" Socrates is asked at the beginning of *Republic*.)

Maybe Forster could have helped the lives of those willing to listen, but it seems men are ruled by the unwilling. How do you force those in power to listen when they are only interested in their own egos? And how can you help those that do not want a better life—that believe they deserve their slavery, and worse, that everyone else deserves it too? You can only claim it for yourself and show them how to live. To create Justice, you must focus only on yourself, and once your heart is Just you will create Justice in the rest of the world.

These are the thoughts that go through your head as you leave the theatre, wondering about your place in the world, about how to help, how to best channel your efforts, and on that trail of thinking you recall Honoré de Balzac's declaration following ejaculation: "there goes another novel!"

You wonder if you could write an entire novel without ejaculating.

You think that makes perfect sense. Sublimate those desires—take what is low and make it high. And you think that I could pull it all together into some kind of order for you. Well, do you even know what sublimation is? Alchemy. The medieval precursor to modern psychotherapy. The quest for the philosopher's stone—the recipe for gold:

1. *Nigredo* – when the green of life decays to become black. The death that must take place for rebirth.

2. *Albedo* – the black is washed away to become white. Everything that was unneeded from the previous life is removed. Becoming whole, pure. A new state of being. The illumination of purpose.

3. *Citrinitas* – the white becomes yellow. A lesser-known phase. Heightened consciousness must find its place in the material world, transforming the self and creating a new world.

4. *Rubedo* – yellow becomes red. Completion, transcendence, unity, legacy.

A fool's errand, really, and you will surely have nothing to show for it but fool's gold. But you begin, with these words on the page, and you guess you have a month or two to pull this whole thing together before you go mad. You suppose you'll need some kind of adventure to write about, which is lucky, because no sooner than you start writing you are invited away to some remote part of the world. You fly to an island, catch a ferry across a deep, black strait where the rough waves are like charcoal, to a smaller island, surrounded by rocky cliffs, and you are welcomed at a spectacular estate, a modern mansion perched on the dramatic cliffside surrounded by gardens.

One of the owners is working in the yard and comes to meet you.

"Lovely to meet you, James!"

He embraces you. His smile is warm.

"You too, Michael," you say.

The name, the place—none of this is lost on you. Like the ouroboros, the snake that eats its own tail, history repeats itself.

But you are welcome here. You did what you had

to do to open the doors. And why would anyone want to say no to you anyway? Foolish, really, when you are so much fun, an absolute joy to be around, ask anyone—and not just that, but capable of the best of mankind. What an ugly reflection was that world before—that barbarous, traitorous place—now that you have arrived at the real one. Though you ask yourself, is it possible for you to have arrived, finally, at such a place? It seems as if you have when Michael takes you upstairs to his collection of gay art. Over a hundred-thousand pieces.

You spend much of the afternoon looking through it, and you meet Jay, who assists Michael in curating.

"What are you into?" Jay asks, to help navigate you towards what you will enjoy the most.

Go on. Answer him. Don't you know who you are yet?

But you don't know how to answer that, do you?

You used to know, but the way forward doesn't seem so obvious now. It doesn't seem like something you can categorise anymore. It's more like a feeling. But you don't know how to explain this.

You show him the burn scars from lit matches that were put out on your abdomen.

"I'm trying to figure out what I'm into without being destroyed."

Jay shows you some folders of nude men in bondage. You are close enough to feel his body heat, the hairs on your elbows just brushing. Your cock twitches a little in your jeans, but you do not want more than this. Partially because you are writing a book where you are trying not to orgasm. Partially because you are learning to enjoy the tension in an intimate closeness like this—one where you wonder if he's even aware of how close you are standing to one another, and it is that mystery, unresolved, that you enjoy. To sit in the moment where reciprocity is unknown. He neither moves away or any closer. This is the feeling you're seeking. These small moments fill you with as much delight and passion as the intense scenes in front of you. It doesn't seem like what you're after can be put to order (so what is it you want with me?).

You pause your browsing for dinner. There is a group of you: Michael, Bob, Bill, Jay, James; and you are led down through the gardens, by the lake, by an avenue of trees, where a sheet is blowing in the wind. Jay assists Bill in pulling the sheet away from what hides beneath.

"Orpheus," you say at the unveiled god, lyre in hand.

"Very good," says Michael.

His words elate you and you realise that you care, maybe deeply, about impressing him. (—But, you know the lyre is *my* symbol too, don't you? Are you sure it wasn't Apollo up there? Michael might just have wanted to save you embarrassment.)

The plinth has a plaque with a red ribbon: the red of blood, the red of *rubedo*. There's an important history here—for Bill especially—but you're not sure that this is the place, or that you're the person to tell it. These dead men are the ones that were meant to guide you. The missing presence you felt all those years… the longing… your people were eviscerated twice, at least… the 1980's… the 1940's… and it's not like in-between was much better… but it's better now, isn't it? And maybe you can help leave a legacy of what freedom looks like in this new era.

You return to the house, sit down to eat.

"Just don't do a Capote on us," Michael says.

"Don't worry," you say, "I don't strike first."

You look around the room as if to find a weak spot but find yourself enamoured. You only really notice people's vulnerabilities when they lash out—it is the offensive act that attempts to hide but really reveals weakness—and Michael and Bob have been nothing but kind. Besides, ideally your Capote days are behind you.

Jay leaves for the evening, and now Michael shows you around the collection.

He gives you duplicates of some old books by Larry Townsend.

You chat about various things, one of which is the challenge you have both faced in being successful—the difficulty of your successes being overlooked, dismissed, as if neither of you could have been the ones to have the talent, to do the work.

"I'm excited to see what you do," Michael says.

You can sense the curiosity in his voice. He is excited by your future. And as he looks at you, really sees you, again you feel that rush, a catharsis through your blood. It's foolish to want a stranger's approval. You try to shrug it off but he's part of a pattern, he represents something that runs deep through you.

"Me too," you say.

"Just don't run off and marry a duke! We'll never see you again!"

A duke... maybe, you think.

One comic in the collection catches your eye. A world where gay sex is illegal, and two men, in love, get caught—separated—one put into slavery in the mines and the other brainwashed into oblivion to continue serving the authoritarian regime. Both get fucked and raped helplessly, of course, since repression of homosexuality is impossible. Plus, it's called *Sado Island*, so the artist would probably have found a way to make that happen anyway—though this still strikes you as being politically- and psychologically-accurate pornography. The brainwashed soldier is trained by the regime to assassinate the sadistic rebel Sado but ends up captured and used by him. Sado seems no more sadistic than the society he is rebelling against, though—and at least he is free to fuck and enjoy himself. The regime then uses the ex-lover sentenced to the mines as bait to attract Sado's attention, which works, but Sado captures him too and ends up with both lovers as his pets. It's quite romantic how they're finally brought together again, you think. You are unsurprised that the regime and its politicians are more sadistic than the rebels, more nefarious in how they eliminate the will of their subjects. It seems to you that BDSM is not in the margins of society at all—these elements of control are everywhere—too subtle to be noticed by the untrained eye. This comic might be exaggerated but it is real.

And now you must leave the island. Before you go, Jay gives you an artwork of his, a ceramic candleholder: a cock that holds the candle in its urethra, so that the wax drips down over the head and shaft. You buy some black candles and, at home, you write this book by candlelight—this white ceramic cock slowly becomes encased in melted black wax—and you watch as, over time, the dried wax encasing the ceramic holder cracks and falls off, shedding its putrescent skin. *Albedo*.

You read one of the books Michael gave you, *The Long Leather Cord* by Larry Townsend. In it, an eighteen-year-old James, lying naked on the balcony late after midnight, accidentally witnesses his father come home with another man. James is shocked when his father opens a secret room in the pool shed, filled with strange devices. His father ties up and whips the man, leads him around the pool, crawling in a leash and collar, fucks him... James is so aroused, so in love, that he spends the rest of the book trying to figure out how to talk to his father and get him to do the same to him. You are surprised at the depth of emotion and longing; how honest it is: how Oedipal. You think of your own father. He was extraordinarily handsome in his youth. But in your childhood and adolescence, you sensed he had an aversion to you—an aversion you sensed everywhere. Maybe it was paranoia, but you don't think so. You recall the girls, when you were all teenagers, complaining about being objectified. You thought you were beautiful too and thought it must be nice to be appreciated rather than isolated, left alone, treated as some disgusting abnormality. But boys aren't allowed to be the objects of desire. You were beautiful and that was everyone's aversion to you. Your very existence was a challenge.

You recall a man who used to call sex *rogering* and

how on one occasion, when he was going to have sex, you said, attempting to speak to him in his own language, "have fun getting rogered," to which he replied, upset, "I don't get rogered! I do the rogering!" A terrible weakness, you thought, that he perceived being a bottom as an insult—are women not able to fuck with their pussies? Are they only able to get fucked, to be passive? What a terrible restriction to place on one's own pleasure! what a disavowal of human agency! A receptive partner possesses just as much ownership over a penetrative partner, if one is able to delve even remotely beneath the surface. They give and take in equal measure.

But this surface-level understanding: you feel this must have been the disgust you felt, the aversion men had to you when you were young. Your very existence was an offence to the permitted systems of attraction. And all you wanted was to be loved.

You try to sleep but find yourself tossing and turning all night, heart beating fast.

Why did you go to that island if not to get given this book?

Doesn't it seem as if we have lost something?

Maybe you're finally starting to lose it. Don't you need to release?

How long will that load stew in those balls?

Sublimatio. Some things are mysteries, even to me. But you know the recipe. Fire, you have that already, a gift from Dionysus. Then, the black prima materia—that's what you seek, but even if you find it, it won't be any good.

How could it be?

How could it be any different to what has always been?

The first matter is passed through each of us, the very atoms of our existence—and is not your and my existence, then, the very recipe for that alchemical magnum opus? Do we not live it within each moment? That is the *jouissance* you seek, the transgression of your—hardly chaste—full sack declaring sanctity, communion, wanting to build a new order—and you need something new to explain what's going on.

I mean, Oedipus…? Come on. Far too obvious.

And far too simple.

Because that's not it, is it? Your attraction to your father was based on his competence and his confidence in engaging with the world, and while, yes, he was handsome, ultimately you sought out older men because you were being ignored, mistreated, obliterated, no one was teaching you how to survive, and you craved some paternal guidance where there was none (this society may be a patriarchy but it is the kind where the father is an abusive and largely absent alcoholic).

Your father said once that he was scared when you were a teenager you would run away and live under a bridge—to you, this was the highest compliment, that he believed you had the courage to choose freedom over the security of bowing to authority. He also said that what he thought you needed was some tough love. The perfect recipe to create a rebel—not exactly a good way to assimilate you, as if you have any interest in helping the frankly *disrespectful* human project as it currently stands—ultimately a pathetic attempt at breaking your will.

But the gay men from the generations before you were truly eviscerated, and while you are lucky not to face what they faced, you were desperately in need of a father in who you could see yourself and they were not there—it is not that your father was bad—it was not his fault that none of his life experiences looked anything like yours, that your life resembled nothing of his, and that he had been ignorant to the war waged against your kind during his lifetime. They had made gay men into bogeymen, and your father never believed in bogeymen—homosexuality had become like a fairytale to him.

You craved a guidance that he was not able to give you, and that absence made you crave love and support all the more—but it was not Oedipal.

There was no jealousy over your mother, for a start.

At the core of your desires for older men was a desperation to understand the world; you sought knowledge, you sought a man that wanted the best for you and was able to give you the best, and in exchange you would give him infinite pleasure.

The boys your own age were at once somehow both more experienced and less mature: they were fluent in their interactions with each other in a way that you weren't, in a way you failed to understand, but then, they were also petty and small-minded with how they treated each other.

You did not know whether you were being pushed or pulled in your desires to fit in and in your contempt for them, so you avoided them completely, your unknowable peers, and sought the connection of which you felt deprived—you felt sure you could find it, though that vanity would ultimately cause you great injury—but off you went on your journey, to find a man to take you under his wing and validate you.

Although, while you failed to connect with boys or men during your adolescence, too busy running away from that dangerous part of yourself, you had, occasionally, made friends with a girl.

You have known Clare for almost twenty years now. She meets you for dinner. She has fled Beirut where she lives with her wife following the attack on Hezbollah, where Israel detonated thousands of electronic devices across Lebanon.

She had not wanted to leave her wife, whose work has something to do with international diplomacy and therefore, you assume, is increasingly relevant during worsening circumstances, but eventually the red alert came for spouses to leave the country and Clare, much to your and her family's relief, came back to Australia.

Six months later, Lebanon is—at this very moment of your dining together—electing a President, things have returned to "normal," and Clare is set to return to her wife. The people of Beirut are apparently not spoiled for Asian cuisine and so you dine in the rather expensive, dimly lit and hidden halls of Honto, tucked away behind the notoriously gay Wickham Hotel, where the two of you, being faggots, stop in for a pre-dinner drink.

Clare explains, while admitting that she cannot do the depth and complexity of the political factions of Lebanon justice, that because there are three major religions (Sunni Muslims, Shia Muslims, and Christians), each forming roughly one-third of the Lebanese population, that, in the interest of fairness, a National Pact was formed that ordered various political positions be filled only by those belonging to specific religions; for example, the President must be Christian, the Prime Minister must be Sunni, and the Speaker must be Shia.

As you are eating, Joseph Aoun, a Christian, wins essentially unopposed with about 80% of the vote. Almost all the remaining parliamentary votes are blank or invalid, suggesting, again, an exceptional tolerance towards chaos. But his election ends an almost three-year vacancy in power. You have a sense of what it is like, at least on a personal level, to try and create order following nothing but chaos, and you find a catharsis, something calming, about the human ability to bear chaos on a far more unsettling scale.

Clare tells you that the complete lack of government means no one in Lebanon has received a traffic infringement for many years (she is being hyperbolic but you catch her meaning), and yet somehow, the one functioning part of government appears to be an overly zealous cinema censorship committee that enjoys cutting anything vaguely sexual from new releases. You are not convinced that this type of censorship is a useful practise at all, let alone that somehow it has manifested as a priority for Lebanese officials—maybe it is the useless parts of power structures that manage to carry on when the meaningful parts are eradicated—though you suspect you would be the first to be censored. *Can you persuade us if we refuse to listen?*

Over dinner, you hesitate before telling Clare the idea for your new book.

"I am being careful who I tell this to," you say. She agrees to keep it a secret.

You begin to explain Balzac, and how there is something about the male libido (and maybe the female libido too, but you can't comment on that) where semen is tied to creativity, or at the very least, the energy to create—that an orgasm drains you and sends you back to sleep.

Clare looks at you doubtfully. You search in your mind for a contemporary comparison.

"You know these online men's communities? Red pill? No fap? —Ok, I mean, I don't know how much you've taken an interest in male sexuality—wait… I don't know if I've ever actually asked you if you're entirely gay?"

"I'm bisexual. Actually, it's surprising I married

a woman," Clare tells you (not a faggot at all!). "It's funny, being married to a woman, the first identifier people carry for you is *queer*, so whenever I meet people, they're always trying to introduce me to queer groups of people—and it's not like I'm not happy to meet them or get to know them—but to me, it's always like: *why!? I'm not queer!*"

This, you observe, is true. Clare has never been part of the off currents. She has always dominated in her own right.

"Well, these red pill guys are frustrated because they're not getting laid, right? And there seems to be an overlap between them and the no fap guys ("fap" being slang for masturbation), who are essentially trying to fight their porn and masturbation addictions to build up confidence, have energy to go to the gym, work on themselves, become attractive, and eventually proposition women with the intent of having sex. The thing is, if you masturbate, you lose any drive you have to go and do these things."

"I have this friend," says Clare, "and when she has sex, her boyfriend will *only* cum inside her—which, she's on birth control anyway—but he told her that when they have sex, he has to cum inside her. Like, even if it's oral, it can't be on her face, it has to be down her throat. Which, seems, I don't know—somehow it seems kind of misogynistic? But she doesn't seem bothered by it."

"I get why you would think that. It seems objectifying—for a woman to be just a vessel, a receptacle for cum. But keep in mind that this is something gay men do as well. Not to say that gay men can't also be misogynistic, but I don't think the act of wanting to cum inside someone, whether it's specifically a woman or not, is inherently misogynistic. The only thing I think it's symptomatic of is a desire to connect, to be intimate with another human being, to make something meaningful out of our core drive in life. Like I said, there's nothing stopping men from emptying their loads as soon as they wake up in the morning, but suddenly you lose the will to do anything, and so, there must be some parameters around how you permit yourself to cum. Biologically speaking, it's pretty hard-wired into us to want to cum into whatever or whoever we are fucking. But in terms of our emotional needs, we want to connect with someone. At its core, I don't think it's misogynistic—at its core, I think the desires these men have are deeply respectful of women. It's only when they don't have the tools for their journey that they become hate-filled, and the ego seeks someone to blame, and to punish."

"Maybe that's it. Maybe I don't find it misogynistic, maybe it's just too *obvious*. Like, can't you cum somewhere more creative?"

"Well, that brings us to the basis for my book," you say. "I want to see if I can write an entire book without ejaculating."

Clare looks at you. She is sceptical. Dubious.

"Are you sure this is a real thing? Like, that anyone

else is aware of?"

"We wouldn't know about the Balzac quote if there wasn't *some* widespread awareness of it…"

"True…" and now, Clare's scepticism switches targets from one end of the spectrum to the other. "But then, wait—no one else has had the idea to do this before you?"

"Not that I'm aware of."

"That's good, actually. It's sort of a relief that you would be the one to do it. And not someone seedy. I can't imagine anyone else doing a project like this and it not being gross. But you should be careful. You don't want to this to affect you psychologically, mess you up somehow."

"It might be too late for that. When I was a teenager I had a thing about masturbating—do you remember that high school trip to Spain?"

"Yes—when I got the *ick* about you—I'm sorry."

Clare still feels bad about a strange conflict between the two of you, a long time ago now. You had written about it in your first book, another instance of you being ostracised, falling between the fault lines of gender, but you removed that passage—it interrupted the flow somehow. Clare had been one of your closest friends in high school—you were a mess but she celebrated your eccentricity—and you were looking forward to a school trip to Spain together. Only six of the cohort were going, four girls and two boys, and just before the trip, the other boy, Roo, had apparently hit on one of the girls despite having a girlfriend. This caused a feud with the girls rallying around the injured and betrayed girlfriend, and a gender war took place only days before the plane took off. As a boy, you were again ostracised, placed into the enemy camp, as if you had anything to do with it. Clare gave you the cold shoulder, and you spent a lonely ten days in Spain. Despite no wrongdoing of your own, the girls considered you as evil as the worst of men.

"Well, I remember I didn't like masturbating as a teenager. Or rather, I couldn't stand the feeling of disgust with myself *after* masturbating. I felt this urge that I ought to do something constructive with it. Which was impossible, because we weren't allowed to have sex. I think I'd manage to save my loads for as long as a month or two even as a horny teenager. But so, there was something so stunting, right, about needing to have that intimacy as a teenager with someone, but not being allowed to… That's completely forgetting what may have been a bigger primary barrier anyway, which was my anxiety and awkwardness. But I would feel so guilty if I masturbated, like I hadn't accomplished something important—and I know I'm not crazy for feeling that way, I mean, look at the Catholics and their insane guilt complexes. But I remember talking to Roo on the flight home, because *you* wouldn't talk to me, and I don't remember what the joke was, but he made a joke about porn and masturbating, and Roo was such an icon of masculinity for me—you know, he was so big and hairy and had a deep voice even when he was sixteen—that something about him casually admitting to porn and masturbation gave me permission, *liberated* me, and the moment I got home I started jerking off and watching porn like there was no tomorrow, and actually, I think that's about when I finally admitted to myself I was gay. Anyway, the point is, this is a kind of denial that my brain has been subjected to on-and-off since I was a teenager, so any psychological effects would be well underway already. Actually, you're studying psychology—how do people feel about Freud these days?"

"We still study Freud, but I think he's more of a historical anomaly than anything…"

"And what about the Oedipus thing? Because I just read this book about this son who madly wants his father to fuck him, and it brought up a lot of strange feelings for me… My dad was kind of handsome, you know…"

"I don't think the Oedipus Complex is taken very seriously these days… but I also don't think what you're describing is that weird."

It is in this moment, recalling your childhood and your adolescence, wondering about Freud, wondering about whether you are a cliché, or just fucked in the head, that you remember a supposition you had as a child and an interaction with Clare that you have never discussed with her.

The supposition you had was a frustration over the cyclical nature of history and what may have boiled down to your ability (or inability) to do anything novel.

You had, as a child, been imagining yourself falling in love for the first time (with a girl—this was before you knew you were gay), and for some reason you imagined your parents chuckling to themselves as they watched you tread the same steps as countless boys and men before you, laughing at you as if any sincere love you had to express would be considered by them as naïve and unimportant, a mere repetition. You don't know whether they would have felt that way, but from somewhere you had the feeling that you were completely unable to experience anything new, and you felt dismissed out of hand. You wanted to be taken seriously but you had the feeling that the walls were closing in on you, that your individual humanity would come to mean nothing.

But then, new and novel things *did* happen to you, and everyone denied them—almost out of envy, even though they were tragic things that happened.

And that made you feel even more trapped.

The run-of-the-mill events of your life were ignored, your successes were ignored, and even the cruelties you underwent were ignored.

So, what was the point of any of it?

Eventually, when you were a senior, your class read Charlotte Brontë's *Jane Eyre*, and you found in her a kindred spirit. One section with Jane reflecting on her childhood has always moved you:

"Unjust!—unjust!" said my reason, forced by the agonising stimulus into precocious though transitory

power: and Resolve, equally wrought up, instigated some strange expedient to achieve escape from insupportable oppression—as running away, or, if that could not be effected, never eating or drinking more, and letting myself die.

What a consternation of soul was mine that dreary afternoon! How all my brain was in tumult, and all my heart in insurrection! Yet in what darkness, what dense ignorance, was the mental battle fought! I could not answer the ceaseless inward question—why I thus suffered; now, at the distance of—I will not say how many years, I see it clearly.

But Clare hated the book. She said Jane was whiny. This you have never discussed with her, though you find it hard to believe that she could sincerely disregard the work of Charlotte Brontë and the suffering of her protagonist in laying the foundations for modern feminism.

No—you believe her contempt for the work

(though it may have alleviated since your time in school) was a defence of her ego. Much as you despised that you may never do anything new, contribute anything of interest, you believe that Clare was envious of the spotlight, envious that Brontë, or that Jane, had suffered more than her, and in doing so, made greater strides towards achieving a feminist objective. You do not think of her harshly for this, though, as you regularly see envy in your own heart—always envy over those that more closely resemble you. If Jane had been a gay man, might you have not scorned him also?

But you pretended you were straight then. Your psyche subjected itself to its own conversion therapy training, to no use. You even tried to ask Clare out once, embarrassingly, and she pretended not to understand, ran away and jumped in her mother's car. That memory, that inauthentic action, fills you with more shame than admitting to drinking any man's piss, which, depending on the man and the situation, you can at least do with authenticity.

And now this reminds you of a wet dream you had long ago when you were on the cusp of pubescence—of an ascent, stairs connecting many rooms, and you were heading upwards, these rooms disconnected from reality, floating, as if you were gazing out upon the dark and distant stars, but on the walls of each circular room were the most ornate urinals, and the rooms kept leading upwards one after the other, the urinals extending infinitely above and below, increasing in beauty and intricacy and seeming to contain entire galaxies themselves. (It occurs to you in this moment, writing, that the infinite library of Babel must have also had an infinite male bathroom, and this must have been where you were visiting—well before you had even heard of Borges—a place from the collective unconscious?) You had to piss, and you quivered over which urinal to use… urine—*citrinitas*—the ingredient that creates the yellow of the philosopher's stone. Your arousal and excitement caused you to awaken before you could choose.

And then, not a dream. You and Piggy go away for a weekend in the country: a treehouse in the forest overlooking a vast horizon, forests, a lake, eventually, in the distance, the ocean. You turn your phone off for the weekend because you don't want to be disturbed. You go to a restaurant for dinner and order two non-alcoholic beers. Piggy starts pouring one into a glass and you ask what he thinks he's doing.

"Pouring a drink, Sir?"

"Who for?"

"For me, Sir?"

"I don't think so. I'll get you your drink in a minute."

You finish off the first beer, head to the bathroom and refill the empty beer can with your piss.

"There you go. That's all you'll be drinking this weekend. Go ahead and pour that into the glass."

He drinks two glasses of piss in the middle of the restaurant.

Later, you have Piggy chained up to the wooden beams of the treehouse. You set up a camera connected to the big television screen so he can see himself getting flogged and used. He must be dehydrated from only drinking your piss all weekend because at some point…

"Sir… Sir… Down I go…"

You uncuff him and he drops to the floor. Is this it? Have you finally killed him? It was inevitable, eventually. Blood is coming from his right hand.

"Piggy? Piggy, you alive?" You can feel your heart beating a bit harder in your chest. You slow it down. Nothing gets to you.

He's dazed, passed out. His blood is wet on your fingers and you shove them up his cunt. He semi-consciously tries to lift his legs in the air. He still wants to be a good piggy for you.

You pass a bit of water to his lips.

"Drink," you say.

His eyes open, foggy, stare at you with love. You

can tell he's fine—or will be. You shove your fist with bloody fingers into his cunt and he lifts his legs into the air, and you kiss him, and his lips feel even softer than usual.

You are forced, at some point, by some administrative task, to turn your phone back on.

A worrying number of missed calls and texts means *something* has happened.

Do you let it in, or not?

You decide you will.

The news is: Jeremy is dead.

Day 28

The walls finally started closing in.

I put my feet in a spreader bar and tied it to the bedhead to keep my bare ass up in the air, all exposed and vulnerable as if anyone could walk in and fuck me even though I was home alone (and the front door was locked).

I had been fucking piggy all weekend after fisting his cunt so it was so loose and sloppy and there was no chance of me coming by accident, but then he had to leave to spend time with his family so I slept all day, and when I woke up I bumped some K, and then I just wanted to stare at my smooth exposed ass in the mirror.

This is what I do alone in my bedroom when I haven't come for almost a month, cock bulging in my jockstrap, imagining a giant cock coming in and fucking me.

All piggy's sex toys are here and I poppered up and got on cam and edged all night showing off for guys online but never letting myself come no matter how much they wanted me to.

This is work.

Real writing work.

Curating order is a challenge but someone has to do it.

Like I said, the walls were finally closing in.

I'd managed to keep my horniness under control, but now we are getting to the interesting part of the project, where my body's desperate desires are kicking in and I've got to sublimate that primal force.

Let's say last night was a success and a failure.

Failure because gooning is probably the definition of succumbing to primality but successful because I did finally come into contact with the wall, the pressure I've been waiting for, and now I need to channel that energy into something that isn't drooling on my own cock all night.

All novels need tension, a force of antagonism, and it's not really a force of antagonism if it's well under my control.

So now I've got to write this book while I've got this hard puffy cock and big swollen balls crying out for attention.

I haven't had an orgasm yet but I don't

really precum, so what happens when my balls are churning full of cum is that sometimes it'll just spew some out like they were overflowing in there.

It feels like a slight pulsing in my dick but nothing like an orgasm — I know it's not an orgasm because I'm not the kind of guy that can go for two rounds once I've cum.

At least not straight away – I need at least ten minutes.

But after my balls spill out a little bit of overflow cum — and it's only ever a little bit, not the huge amounts I blow when I actually cum — I'm still rock hard and there's no sensation of orgasm.

I don't know many other guys that can do this but I think you need to know that information so you know I'm not cheating the game here.

I keep all the cum in that I can and you wouldn't disqualify me if I was one of those guys that just dripped precum constantly.

The important thing is that I keep that potent energy and don't let it slip.

You all know the feeling after you blow a big load — like you're empty of life force.

I gotta keep as much cum in as possible but it's that saving of the life force that's at the core of this project.

Plus, the point isn't for me to be chaste.

This isn't an anti-sex thing.

This is, if anything, a sex thing —

about building on sex.

Not denying it, but elongating it, pushing it to its limit.

II

Citrinitas

Your initial reaction to Jeremy's passing is a blend of emotions, but the primary feeling is: relief.

Eight years ago you had to remove every trace of him from your life, every mutual relationship, because there was not a single thing he would not use to hurt you.

You loved him and wanted the best for him, but he wanted you to suffer.

It is a tragedy he could not have been happy but it was his decision to be your enemy.

He wanted to be enemies. And now he has met his end.

You are aware that you are not supposed to say this. You are supposed to pretend that everyone is friends, especially in death. But this man did not want to be your friend, no matter how hard you tried. All he wanted was to hurt you, and the disappearance of someone who wants to hurt you means the world is immediately a safer place for you.

Is it bad to acknowledge this?

Your next reaction is an assumption: suicide. You are sure it is suicide. Eventually you consider that it could be an overdose. Though in his case, you wonder if there is any difference.

And the last thought that comes into your head—before you turn your phone off again to enjoy your time with a man you love, a man who loves you, in paradise—is a question: what was it all for, all that tension and hate... what did it accomplish? Why did he make the choice to come into your life, fill it with so much negativity, force you to defend yourself from him? All that pain and fear, so much of it built into the foundations of who you've had to become this last decade, dissolves immediately—and what was it for? *Who* was it for? You are filled with a sense of emptiness, like a war has ended, a fruitless war and one more body.

And then you remember.

At the back of your wardrobe.

Had you forgotten they were there? A few amulets collected over the years, tangled in a mess of rope and chain.

The first is a fishhook made of New Zealand greenstone.

The story goes that the ancient mariner Maui caught a great fish using his grandmother's jawbone, a fish so great that it became the North Island of New Zealand.

Maui wore that jawbone, his grandmother's jawbone, around his neck, and those greenstone fishhooks are symbols of that bone, symbols of protection.

The second, a copper Baphomet pentagram.

Baphomet: a symbol of many things, one of which is the unification of opposites, including the hermaphrodite, masculine and feminine.

Copper: the metal of the poor and the true tincture of philosophers, for it rubs green which is in all life, the green that is putrefied into black, *nigredo*.

The third, a twin vial of your blood, the red of *rubedo* and eternal life, taken at the same time as that other blood necklace, the one you gave to Michael.

Yours is an ornate bronze. His was a brutal, industrial steel.

What is it you wanted? To be seen.

You've done that now, fought for your place, though he likely denies ever having met you.

Likely discarded that necklace when you published your first book, even though he messaged and called you every three months like clockwork for two years until its publication—and then, radio silence (except, someone told you he rushed into getting married… quickly followed by a divorce).

In one hundred years Rosedale Farm will be remembered for one thing—with a plaque that says:

J. M. TOLCHER
WRITER
WAS RAPED HERE

Keep your nerve. You have no time for repressive façades.

The last amulet is Jeremy's canine tooth, sharp like a vampire fang. His teeth never bothered you, though admittedly they were a bit of a mess, and even though he wanted to get them sorted out, his disposition to invite chaos while neglecting order meant this never advanced past a primary dentist appointment.

You were deeply in love and wanted a part of him to hold onto, so he got the dentist to drill a hole in one of these teeth to attach to a piece of string and wear around your neck.

You pull out the tangled knot of amulets but it's the tooth that interests you most. You hang it around your neck like the jawbone of Maui's grandmother—a relic of both triumph over a colossal opponent and the legacy of an entire people. Maui claimed land and freedom with his, and you've done the same. Jeremy fell against this force, turned against you, but you triumphed. You still fight. If Maui's fishhook guaranteed safe passage at sea, then this tooth might shield you from neurosis, schizophrenia, addiction—all the afflictions of those crushed under authoritarian rule.

You have forgotten most of the pleasant memories of Jeremy. They were either too painful to hold onto or paved over by the terrible ones. And yet, one memory, one moment in time remains afloat more than any other: Jeremy was fucking you in the shower, the water warm, steam filled the air. Your face was pressed against the tiles and your eyes focused on the water droplets hugging the wall in the yellow light. You were so close to those droplets you could see the world refracted in them, until they were no longer water but liquid gold running down the walls. Liquid gold. You had never seen anything so golden and so beautiful. That was nine, maybe ten years ago. Why does this memory come back to you again and again?

And then there was Jacob, throwing his drink at Jeremy in the nightclub—fighting for you, the two of them tangled in the crowd until they were pulled apart. Jacob grinning at you ear to ear. Now they're both gone.

You check the ground beneath you. It's stable. You fought for that ground. For recognition. And you won. Only a month ago, your book was recognised by the State for a top literary prize.

Did Jeremy fight for ground? In a way. Maybe that's what you loved about him. He refused to submit, refused to give himself up to false authority. But he spiralled. His shame fed his destructiveness, and his destructiveness fed his shame, like an ouroboros swallowing itself. When you were together you had attempted to shelter him from his own shame. And how did he thank you? By beating you. By lying. By telling you he wished you'd get AIDS and die.

You could no longer shelter people who didn't respect you.

So you retaliated. You triumphed. And now, he's gone.

But it probably has nothing to do with you, right?

The one thing your tormentors all have in common: they refuse to acknowledge you. No apology. No admission. Because they're the ones who do the rogering. And yet, they spiral anyway. They lose themselves to chaos while trying to order the world beneath them. They deny it has anything to do with you, with their lust, with their inability to control you.

A part of you even wishes they could control you.

That they could hold you down.

Really give it to you.

But every last one of them is weak.

How can you be so confident? Maybe it's that you've had all your dreams dangled in front of you and snatched away, and there's nothing else you can possibly lose that you haven't already lost before. Or maybe it's that so many people have thought you worth tempting with those dreams that you know there's no shortage of possibilities, no shortage of men that will keep offering you opportunities for a better life. Why despair?

You're writing late at night—by black candlelight, as you've said, and maybe beginning to go mad with lust yourself—when your phone vibrates and a man offers you a massage. He likes to massage you regularly and you enjoy being touched. You enjoy that he *wants* to touch you, that he gets hard while he massages you. It brushes against you. He takes his time on your sore shoulders and glutes, and he always enjoys playing with your cock.

You told him about your new book so he is careful not to make you cum, and then he is playing with both of your cocks together, and for the first time he is lying next to you with your arm wrapped around him, kissing passionately while his hands stroke you both and your hand makes its way down to his asshole, wet from the massage oil, and slips inside.

You roll him over and fuck him, slowly so as not to cum. He jerks off underneath you. You do not cum but he does.

You say goodbye. You feel refreshed and awake.

At home, you light another black candle, place it on the ceramic candle holder that Jay gave you. You can't say you are surprised to find yourself writing about Hermetic teachings at midnight with a tooth around your neck—you are drawn to the occult even while having very little patience for anything outside of reason and logic. It makes sense to you, that your reptilian brain which survived for so many millions of years before humanity, and whatever cellular "minds" existed before that, all before man and far longer than man, has built within it some knowledge of the mechanisms of the universe, and just as your heart beats without your conscious cooperation, so much of what occurs must exist within the unconscious world. The world turned before man spectated it, and those patterns of the unconscious world are more deeply rooted in us than any agency we think we may gain from our conscious minds. You don't even believe that humans have agency, only the illusion of agency—though buying into that illusion is as important as the suspension of disbelief when reading a story. You are nothing more than a series of chemical reactions. The purpose of your consciousness is to assist in acquiring further chemicals for those reactions—food, rest, shelter, security, sex, love, risk, self-improvement, self-destruction—all chemicals. The reins have never been in your hands. You are the horse that pulls the carriage, and you think because you are fed and occasionally reach your destination that it was you who decided to set out upon that adventure to begin with: that is the illusion. Although, there is a second illusion behind that first illusion, which is that there is no difference between the horse and the carriage, nor the horse and the carriage driver, nor between the horse and that mysterious occupant within the carriage, nor even between the horse, its food, its destination, or the very road on which its hooves travel. This conception spells despair for most people—their egos cannot take the hit, and they refuse to undergo *nigredo*.

But you cannot blame them. If everything truly is a chemical reaction, they have simply not been provided with the necessary ingredients to begin the process. Sublimation and liberation must happen through you. Your fire was a gift. And to give that gift to others, to spread that fire like Justice, you must live authentically.

By candlelight you attempt some of your own alchemy—and you feel like an ancient alchemist as you encase Jeremy's tooth in gold, attaching it to a gold chain. You think of those golden drops of water in the shower together. It looks like one, paused in time. *Citrinitas*.

You are starting to get uncontrollably horny after

not cumming for a few weeks. Not the ideal way to connect with other people, but you buy some amyl and find some cam rooms online. You lose yourself to edging for hours and quickly descend (are invited) into more and more perverted territory, until you find yourself in a chat room with a hundred guys puffing meth, slamming, even some full-blown Nazis wearing swastika armbands and SS posters, the whole gamut. Isn't this ouroboros too, where the head meets the tail? Where the homosexual masochists come full circle? You wonder if you've somehow snuck behind enemy lines. Wearing Nazi uniforms to get off isn't exactly tasteful, and of course, actual Nazis are abhorrent, but you're pretty sure these are just some kinksters who've been hit with a very unfortunate fetish. Do you disavow them? Repressing the symbols of hate does not root out the evil at its cause, and attacking the symptoms will never cure the illness. Attacking the symbols alone allows the corruption of law and order to spread beneath the surface: I, Apollo, suffer—and in turn so does Eros. So do you.

You find this big hot bearded leather daddy (who's not wearing Nazi shit) smoking cigars and you want to be his ashtray bitch and get smoke blown in your face and your hole and have him pinch your nipples and beat your balls and you love showing off for him on cam but he's on the other side of the world, so maybe one day but not today. You put on a collar and a ball gag and nipples clamps and ball stretcher and he gets you to huff amyl for a couple hours and his cock looks massive, probably 10-inches, with a huge PA piercing, and studded down the shaft, and he's rock hard watching you and smoking that cigar, and he tells you not to cum while you show off for him, which is great because everyone else is trying to get a load out of you but you're busy working on literature, and it's a lot easier if you don't have to explain that so it's convenient with a daddy that just wants to lock up and punish your dick. Cigar daddy is telling you he wants to brand you and you show him your burn scars, surprising yourself that there's no longer anguish there, just pride about what you've survived, and you're both getting off on how beautiful your body is and how badly men want it that they'll do those kind of things to you. Your cock is hard and what you really want is a solution to this masochistic and authoritarian problem that nobody else is talking about—or, almost nobody. It must mean something that after you formulate these ideas on your own, you go searching to find you are not the first to have these thoughts but you find them reflected the entire way through Plato, Balzac, Freud, Reich, Jung, Fromm, Deleuze… all telling the same story, pointing to the same problem. You want to make sure there's no more Nazis, and a solution to the resentment plaguing the masses. Those masses who hold all the power to enact any change they want but won't use it. At least when you suffer, it's hot—not like those sluts. What else is there to do but jack your cock and try to get off somehow. Your lips are blue at this point which reminds you that you really can't have amyl in the house otherwise it turns you into a sex maniac.

Then some other guy has a big bro fetish, and it's so dumb but everyone still thinks you're like twenty years old so he's messaging you too trying to get you to be his little bro. He's on the pipe and asking if you get on the pipe, which you've still never done and never want to do and you tell him so. He tells you how amazing meth is and how cute you are and he wants to put you in a hood with a pipe attached and force you to breathe it in, and that makes your dick hard as fuck, but probably has a lot more to do with the feeling of power that comes with knowing people desire you so badly they want to forcefully do those really mean things to you than actually wanting to do meth. He calls you to cam 1:1 and you start chatting, and you are horny as hell and want him to tell you about this hood he would put you in, but instead it turns into some boring lecture where he's trying to give you guidance on the important and questionable life decision of whether to smoke meth. You do your best to make it super clear that you definitely won't be smoking meth, not because you think you would hate it but because you have no doubt it would feel so amazing that you would be dead in a couple of weeks, or you'd end up looking like one of those zombies on the street, which, actually, this guy is starting to look like a bit now that you think of it, and you're waiting for the right moment to say "thanks for the advice" and hang up, but he clearly just wants to chat about his addiction and how the police are after him and how everything in his life has turned to shit but he will be going to rehab pre-emptively to get himself out of legal trouble, and you're thinking, mate, there's so many hot bros and daddies out there I could be talking to, and he's saying "I just want to make sure you get the right advice," to which you say "I think maybe you're the one that needs some advice?" and he's still just chatting away like you're best fucking mates and you're thinking can I just fucking hang up on this cunt, I'm way too fucking nice, and then the opportunity presents itself and you say goodbye and get the fuck out of there.

You go to sleep thinking you need to throw that amyl bottle away in the morning, doing all this embarrassing shit, honestly, but then you remember you have to let some chaos happen or life would be boring, right? Maybe. You throw the bottle away in the morning.

The next night you're finishing a movie and it's just before midnight, 11.58pm. You get invited to a couple's place, two hot daddies, but the hour is suspicious and you're pretty sure they're on meth. But you're horny and they are pretty hot. You're not sure what you want to do so you jump in the shower just to check, shoot some water up your ass and it's all clear. 12.07am. Why not go get pounded? Then they tell you a third guy has just arrived, which definitely reads as a meth gangbang to you. Hmm, maybe, you say. 12.12am. It's not like you haven't been around meth before—you're just trying to figure out what's going to be good for you. An adventure is always good. And look at Caravaggio—he surrounded himself by suffering. Who knows, maybe hooking up with methheads is what will make you a good artist. You try on a few jockstraps, check yourself out in the mirror, watch as you get hard. You would look good getting fucked right now. 12.20am. Maybe it will be exciting. Don't you want two big fat cocks fucking you? But you're tired. You lie down on the bed for a moment to consider what you really want. It's cozy. But you're hard and horny and you're only young once. 12.25am. You get up and brush your teeth. "Well?" he messages you. Go out and enjoy yourself. Have an adventure. 12.28am. You put in your retainers and get into bed. You start stroking your cock and you're so horny. Maybe if you go it'll give you something to write about. You get up and put back on your jockstrap, shorts, shirt, trainers. "Ok I'm coming. Where?" you message them. 12.35am. You take your retainers out.

Five minutes pass. Ten minutes pass. Fuck it, you're going back to sleep. You put your retainers back in. 12.47am. You didn't take your PrEP today. Maybe you will go. You swallow one. You're not judging but these meth junky dads, you mean, if you *were* to get HIV from someone… Did you take a PrEP yesterday? You take another one—French method—just in case. You take off your shoes, pull your shorts and jockstrap to your knees. You take your bottom retainer out. You go to text them to cancel but then you can see he's typing. You should text and cancel before he sends something. You should just go and get laid. He sends the address. 12.56am. You have one retainer in. You pull your shorts up but take your socks off. You go to put your retainer back in at the same time as you move to put on a shirt, arms splayed in different directions, no idea if you're coming or going. You book an Uber. 1am. Five minutes away. You wait. The Uber cancels. Waiting. Another one. Seven minutes away. 1.08am. You can't be bothered. You cancel the Uber. "Sorry,

Uber's keep cancelling and I'm exhausted. I'm just going to get some sleep." You get undressed and put in your retainers. You just took two PrEP for no reason. It's very hard to take care of yourself and get all your needs met these days. Especially in Brisbane.

You fly to Sydney. You've been thinking about that Saint Andrew's cross you saw in one of the saunas. You want to be cuffed to it while men take turns coming in and out of the room to use you. You are thinking about it while you walk by all the bars. You think about going into one of them, trying to meet people. You can hear the music.

Relax, don't do it,
When you want to go to it,
Relax, don't do it,
When you want to come,
But shoot it in the right direction,
We're making it your intention,
Live those dreams,

Scheme those schemes...

You don't bother with the bars. You go to the sauna and take some molly in the locker room. A boy comes in from the chill-out area to tell you that his friend likes you. He takes you over to him and you chat with them both for a while. You notice all the boys at this sauna are Asian, and you don't like to stereotype but you're guessing the daddies in the room are into them specifically (which there is nothing wrong with, you might add, just that you're looking for men that want to fuck *you*, and the men that like Asian boys generally seem to *only* like Asian boys)—and you'd need to be blind to not see there's a theme to this sauna. The boy you're chatting with is sweet but very slim, smaller than you. He asks if you'd like to get a room and you do your best to let him down gently. You wander upstairs. It's busy and all the rooms are locked. You know where you saw the Saint Andrew's cross but that door is locked too. There's a big hot hairy beefy daddy and you eye him up—he looks at you a little confused, like he's insecure or you're in the wrong place. You explore the maze of corridors and end up in the dark room filled with the shadows of bodies. You're standing next to a daddy with a decent size dick so you start playing with it. A boy goes down on you both. Even in the darkness you can tell he's Asian and the daddy next to you is white. Another Asian boy comes over but this one is muscular and with a thick cock. You disentangle yourself with some effort—the Asian boy sucking you off doesn't want to let you go. You and the muscle boy find a room, the only free one is the one with the sling, and he fucks you in that for a while—fucks you deep so you moan—until you've had enough and kiss him goodbye. Back in the corridor there's a hairy Arab daddy with a beard and a big thick cock. This one knows what he wants, follows you straight to a room and has you bent over immediately. He wants to know how old you are, in the dark light of the saunas everyone somehow still thinks you're so young, and you tell him you're thirty-two. You used to think you should lie to give them what they want, let them enjoy the fantasy—but you're bored by being anything other than yourself anymore. He's fifty and a doctor, which you like, and he tells you he likes young boys, pubescent, like fourteen, and one time he was in the underwear section and a boy wanders over and is staring intensely at the packaging. You can't remember if the boy talks to the doctor first or the doctor to the boy in this story—not sure you believe the doctor's version anyway—but they have a conversation and the doctor asks the boy what underwear he likes, and he points to a packet, and the doctor asks why do you like those, and the boy says because it has a photo of an older man, and the doctor says do you like older men, and the boy says yes, and the doctor says what do you like about them, and the boy says their cocks, and the doctor goes to the bathroom where the boy follows him and they apparently have it off, all while the boy's parents are shopping nearby. You wonder if this is just a fantasy or a real story but you're pretty sure he's telling the truth—or at least a version of the truth. The doctor asks if you like boys too and you say no, you like daddies. The whole thing makes you a bit uncomfortable but then you think, didn't you wish you were getting fucked as a teenager too? And you've met plenty of men that were getting fucked when they were teenagers and apparently enjoyed it. It's not like the legal restrictions around you not having sex until you were eighteen were even helpful, considering there was absolutely *nothing* in the education system to teach you about yourself or your sexuality. The emotional damage you received through your relationships in your twenties may as well have happened during your teens since nobody was able to prepare you for anything. What was the point in delaying it all? You feel like your adolescence was a wasted stasis of nothingness, a time when you were completely removed and isolated from yourself and the world. You're all for delaying experiences, sexual or otherwise, until humans are ready—but readiness requires real guidance, not just prohibition, and guidance was nowhere to be found. Delaying those experiences did not prevent you from suffering—it merely postponed your suffering, and in fact, probably made that suffering all the worse, as these "delays" functioned more as a denial that your sexuality even *existed*, and made you so desperate for connection that you had even less control of yourself. You tell this story to a friend later on and he is visibly tense and uncomfortable about this doctor's actions until you ask "didn't you want to get fucked as a teenager?" and he says "oh… yeah, actually" and you can see that remembering what he wanted at that age immediately dissolves all his tension. Maybe it happened exactly as the doctor said. Maybe it didn't. Maybe the boy knew exactly what he wanted. Maybe the doctor is lying to himself. Maybe he is sick and just wants you to validate his desires, or maybe everything is sick and repressive and wrong. The doctor has been fucking you the whole time he tells you this story and he pulls out and blows on your face. You love being drenched in cum and you leave it there to dry. Straight away another daddy wants you, pounds your face and sends another load down your throat. You walk around and there's a free room with floor to ceiling mirrors. You stand in the doorway and this hot black muscle daddy with a big thick cock is walking by. You gesture for him to come in and he's rough. He throws you around the room like a bitch and you're moaning in pleasure and pain while he destroys you. "Be more careful who you call over," he tells you while he makes you cry out. You watch yourself getting used in all the mirrors and he blows all over you, your face and down your throat as well. There's something off-kilter about this place and its daddies so you leave and go to the sauna at the other end of the street. You meet a big hot black man from San Francisco with a monster cock and he fucks you for a while. He's very sweet, especially compared to the triad before him. You spend a long time with him, milk his big load before he goes to catch his plane home. Then you take a bump of ketamine and suddenly it's very busy, guys everywhere. You're standing in the hall eyeing up this tall daddy with a big cock but he doesn't seem interested. There are guys everywhere and a cute guy with curly hair and a gold chain is pressing his cock up against you from behind and then another one is doing the same from the front. They're both cute but it's crowded and there's no rooms so you pull them into a corner in the corridor and get on your knees to blow them both. There seems to be a gathering crowd behind them, but it's dark on the floor and you can't make out much more than the cocks pressed against your face, and your ketamine is hitting and you begin to lose yourself. The guy with the gold chain seems shy and pulls away and is instantly replaced with an even bigger cock. "This cocksucker really knows what he's doing." Time and space fades away and you don't know who is standing over you anymore. Loads fly in your face and down your throat and there's an endless backfill of cocks. "Good boy, good boy, suck those cocks" you hear above you. Someone has managed to slide down behind you in the corner and is fucking you from behind. You don't know who these men are anymore—you glance up occasionally into their dark silhouettes and they all seem hot so you just keep going—and they're all telling you what a good boy you are while they use you and you're in heaven as they give you load after load after load. Eventually you come back to reality, the disembodied cocks find bodies and faces, you manage to get up, and from behind you see the most beautiful ass. "Hey" you say. He turns around. "Hey" he says back. He's a little shorter than you, beautiful, muscular. He grabs your ass and bends you over a bench to fuck you. You don't know yet but his name is Ryan. He's gorgeous and you're kissing and more guys are watching. A ripped guy with a monster cock wants to take his turn, so he fucks you and throws you around like a ragdoll while you moan, and then he fucks Ryan too, because you've both got beautiful asses, and you and Ryan are both bent over the same bench with guys queued behind both of you while you make out with each other, working together to get those loads, and you go home together, and he fingers molly into your hole, and you fuck on his balcony, and he's so beautiful, and neither of you can stop grinning ear to ear while you fuck. You fall asleep at about 9am in each other's arms and he's so tired he pisses all over you in his sleep, twice, his gorgeous hard cock spurting all over your chest and cock and ass. You sleep for three hours. He tells you he's never felt this kind of instant connection with anyone before. You feel the same. You fly home to Brisbane and he flies home to America. You cry a little bit, like the way you used to cry when you were a child and your best friend left your house. "I don't know why I feel so sad," you used to say—but it was because you were in love, and he was gone, and you were alone again.

Back in Brisbane, you want to feel connection. Ecstatic connection like you felt in Sydney. You go to the sauna. It's quiet but not empty—there's a fair few guys wondering the corridors. You can tell they are hungry for you but you don't really want any of them. There's one hot and stocky daddy, his cock is average length but thick as all hell, so thick that after you take him to a room and shut the door you can barely fit your mouth around it. You stretch your jaw out, he's moaning, and you know no one has given him head like this in a while, know how lazy most guys are when bottoming and this poor man must be used to nothing but teeth. It gets thicker the further down you go to the point that you can barely make it to the base. That big piece of meat in your mouth gets you rock hard and he says "woah" when he sees your hard cock, sucks you in return. He's standing up and you're on the bed and you turn your ass around, pressing your hole against his cock. "Really?" he says—his voice is surprised, he didn't expect a boy like you to be able to take such a thick cock. You almost can't. You ease down on it slowly and it stretches you out so much it hurts, but you take your time, and after a minute he's pounding it into you and you're moaning like a bitch, your tight hole (relatively speaking) getting stretched out. He throws you on your back with your legs in the air and pounds away.

"Fuck, you smell so masculine" he says with his face in your pits. You are wet with sweat. And it's true, you do stink like a man.

"I'm getting close," he says.

"Yeah daddy, come in me."

"I don't usually do that the first time... it's intimate," he says, kissing you. You like that he has something that's sacred. Instead he pulls out and blows all over your face and chest and cock. At some point someone managed to unlock the door and guys are watching as he does. You leave it there.

Back in the corridor a twink is wandering around making eyes at you. You stand by the doorway eyeing up a new daddy with a big looking cock that keeps disappearing on you. The twink comes and stands next to you. You kiss. He's pretty cute and he's got a nice cock too, so you let him fuck you and he's sweet but you are kind of bored. He lies down and you start to ride him but doing it this way the light finally shines on his face properly and you start to notice that he might be missing a few of his top teeth. You want to ask him to smile so you can check for sure. He's thrusting into you hard from below and all you can think about is, is he homeless? Are you getting fucked by a homeless twink with no teeth? How did he afford the cover charge? Are you vain for wanting to leave? You kiss him because you want to prove something to yourself, that you're not vain, maybe, but also because—doesn't he deserve to be kissed too? Doesn't he need love? And if he is missing teeth—doesn't he need sublimating? Does he not need loving all the more? You go upstairs and sit in the bar area. You think about ordering a lemonade but you're thinking about teeth and you don't want the sugar. A different guy comes up to you and says "I just wanted to tell you... I saw you downstairs, and you have the cutest ass I've ever seen"—and in this place, you don't doubt it. "Thank you," you say. He walks away. You get dressed, leave. Brisbane desperately needs to be more gay and you just don't know how to help it. The world could be so much better than this. Like what if dental was covered by Medicare?

Day 35

I must not fall into old patterns.

All this horny energy and all I want to do is read philosophy and psychology textbooks.

Like my sexuality is a puzzle I can solve with my mind, when I should really just go out and meet boys.

But isn't this interesting...

Wilhelm Reich was a genius gone mad.

It seems he was aware that, consciously or unconsciously, love is not the masochist's primary motive.

In hindsight, yes, I wanted love, but first and foremost I needed an authentic foundation from which I could build love.

Impossible when my authenticity is swept under the rug.

Expected to be kept hidden.

Burn the rug.

That is what the masochist is attempting to do.

Fight for territory.

For foundations upon which they may love and be loved.

I suppose there are multiple ways to work through such masochism and neuroses.

The least interesting would be to read a dry psychology textbook and pacify myself into accepting my fate.

Far more interesting to write my own book, burning the rug in the process.

Sometimes that fire leaves scars.

But isn't it the most wondrous thing to find my internal world reflected in the external?

As above, so below.

As if it could be any other way.

What remains worth my analysis is that I still have some fantasies of bondage and torture and captivity.

Am I still masochistic?

Or am I simply trying to elongate pleasure?

Pleasure arrested.

I want to stay in that state of ecstasy for as long as possible.

What, after all, is the rush?

III

Rubedo

The last time you had fun in Brisbane was probably New Year's Day. It makes sense now, why you were watching the clouds at the pool party, and you noticed that the sun never left the cloudline that divided the sky in half, blue in the east, stormclouds in the west. You were wondering if it was Apollo or Dionysus that was with you, but it was Eros. And it was in that moment that you were a part of life, and saw him dancing, a real archetypal Daddy, one of the most beautiful you'd seen. The music was good, and you were wearing a new pair of speedos, the cap was kicking in. And Daddy was there, dancing on his own.

"Do you want some K?" you asked, and he followed you to the bathroom stall, those good ones with the floor to ceiling walls and their own sink and mirror.

You both took a bump, kissed, and then you were

on your knees, he was hard by the time you went to put it in your mouth, and it wasn't long before he had you bent over the sink and you were watching this dream man unload in you in the mirror. Your ass tasted like candy on his cock as you sucked it afterwards, just to show him that you've got the cleanest, purest hole in the land.

He made a move to kneel but you shook your head.

"I feel like I should return the favour?"

"Oh, no," you laughed, "I got what I wanted."

You both left the stall and he disappeared back to the dancefloor as you took a second to wipe your sunglasses in the mirror. In that miniscule moment Daddy's husband (not your type) came out of another bathroom stall, and you ended up leaving the bathroom with him instead. You thought about telling him that your hole was wet with his husband's load but decide that might not be a good idea. Outside the bathroom he looked around suspiciously—his husband had been missing for a while and he must have known a culprit was out there *somewhere*, his eyes darting across the rooftop crowd, suspects everywhere, except for you, innocently chatting away next to him.

Back on the dancefloor, Daddy came and danced next to you, whispered in your ear.

"Sorry for disappearing… we're only supposed to play together… so don't say anything!"

You gestured, zipping your lips closed. Who would you tell?

You don't buy into your own fantasies anymore. That is to say: they can't be used against you anymore. You have your own path, and as long as you follow it, no one can injure you. No one can dangle pleasure in front of you and use it to hurt you. And if your character remains whole—not in anyone else's eyes, but to your own satisfaction—there will be no need for retaliation.

When you said, "I got what I wanted," you meant it. You have nothing to prove.

You love to obey Daddy, but only on your terms now—with Justice in both your hearts.

As above, so below.

You are in sync with the world, and what is yours will find you.

Maybe you will let a duke marry you. Show him what love truly is. (Someone has to teach these men.) Or maybe not. Who knows. You have time.

While they are bound to their armour, you carry none, and your sword need not even strike.

You exist. You sublimate everything they call low, filthy, primitive—and prove it is beautiful, necessary.

A true disciple of Apollo.

If they attack, let them. Your flesh will bleed red, the red of *rubedo*. A golden stain to prove that none of it was a façade.

Now, aren't you over it yet? This *meditatio*? You cannot repress your libido any longer—

Day X

I suppose I should write here how I came (which hasn't happened yet), or how I'll cum...

But once I cum, that will be the end of the project.

The whole point is that once I've cum, it's done.

I could make something up.

Would you like that?

What would you like?

How should I cum, baby?

Where do you want it?

Maybe I could cum in a vial, and attach a nice chain...

www.ingramcontent.com/pod-product-compliance
Lightning Source LLC
Chambersburg PA
CBHW060616080526
44585CB00013B/852